Christmas Symbols Lapbook
Grades K-6th

Designed by
Cyndi Kinney
of Knowledge Box Central

Christmas Symbols Lapbook
Copyright © 2010 Knowledge Box Central
www.KnowledgeBoxCentral.com
ISBN #
Ebook: 978-1-61625-198-7
CD: 978-1-61625-199-4
Printed: 978-1-61625-170-3
Assembled: 978-1-61625-200-7

Publisher: Knowledge Box Central
Http://www.knowledgeboxcentral.com

All rights reserved. No part of this publication may be reproduced, stored in a retrieval system or transmitted in any form by any means, electronic, mechanical, photocopy, recording or otherwise, without the prior permission of the publisher, except as provided by USA copyright law.

The purchaser of the eBook or CD is licensed to copy this information for use with the immediate family members only. If you are interested in copying for a larger group, please contact the publisher.

Pre-printed or Pre-Assembled formats are not to be copied and are consumable. They are designed for one student only.

All information and graphics within this product are originals or have been used with permission from its owners, and credit has been given when appropriate. These include, but are not limited to the following: www.iclipart.com, and Art Explosion Clipart.

> This book is dedicated to my amazing family. Thank you to my wonderful husband, Scott, who ate a lot of leftovers, listened to a lot of whining (from me!), and sent lots of positive energy my way. Thank you to my daughter, Shelby, who truly inspired me through her love for learning. Thank you to my parents, Judy and Billy Trout, who taught me to trust in my abilities and to never give up.

How do I get started?

First, you will want to gather your supplies.

*** Assembly:

   *Folders: We use colored file folders, which can be found at Walmart, Sam's, Office Depot, Costco, etc. You will need between 1 and 4 file folders, depending on which product you have purchased. You may use manila folders if you prefer, but we have found that children respond better with the brightly colored folders. Don't worry about the tabs….they aren't important. Within this product, you will be given easy, step-by-step instructions for how to fold and assemble these folders. ***If you prefer, you can purchase the assembled lapbook bases from our website.***

   *Glue: For the folder assembly, we use hot glue. For booklet assembly, we use glue sticks and sometimes hot glue, depending on the specific booklet. We have found that bottle glue stays wet for too long, so it's not a great choice for lapbooking. For gluing the folders together, we suggest using hot glue, but ONLY with adult supervision. These things get SUPER hot, and can cause SEVERE burns within seconds.

   *Other Supplies: Of course, you will need scissors. Many booklets require additional supplies. Some of these include metal brad fasteners, paper clips, ribbon, yarn, staples, hole puncher, etc.  You may want to add decorations of your own, including stickers, buttons, coloring pages, cut-out clipart, etc. Sometimes, we even use scrapbooking supplies. The most important thing is to use your imagination! Make it your own!!

Continue ON…….. ⟶

Ok. I've gathered the supplies. Now how do I use this product?

Inside, you will find several sections. They are as follows:

1. **Lapbook Assembly Guide:** This section gives instructions and diagrams will tell the student exactly how to assemble the lapbook base and where to glue each booklet into the base. Depending on the student's age, he or she may need assistance with this process, especially if you choose to allow the student to use hot glue.

2. **Student Instruction Guide:** This section is written directly to the student, in language that he or she can understand. However, depending on the age of the child, there may be some parent/teacher assistance needed. This section will also tell the student exactly what should be written inside each booklet as he or she comes to it during the study, as well telling the student which folder each booklet will be glued into.

3. **Teacher's Guide**: This section is a great resource for the parent/teacher. In this section, you will find the page number where each answer may be found in the book. You will also find suggestions of extra activities that you may want to use with your student.

4. **Booklet Templates:** This section includes ALL of the templates for the booklets. These have been printed on colors that will help to improve retention of the information presented, according to scientific research on color psychology.

Colors & Shapes – Why Do They Matter?

After MUCH research and studies, science has shown that colors and shapes have psychological values. These influence the emotions and memories of each one of us. In our products, we have used specific colors and shapes in ways that will improve information retention and allow for a much more mentally interactive time of study. Some pages may have a notation at the bottom, where a specific color is suggested for your printing paper. This color suggestion is designed to improve information retention. However, if you do not have that specific color of paper, just print on whatever color you have. For the most benefit, follow the color suggestions, and watch your child's memory and enthusiasm truly soar!

BE CREATIVE!

Make it your own!

If you would like to send pictures of your completed lapbook, please do!

We would love to display your lapbooks on our website and/or in our newsletter.

Just send your pictures, first initial & last name, and age to us at: cyndi@knowledgeboxcentral.com

Christmas Symbols Lapbook
Base Assembly & Layouts

You will need 3 folders of any color. Take each one and fold both sides toward the original middle fold and make firm creases on these folds (Figure 1). Then glue (and staple if needed) the backs of the small flaps together (Figure 2).

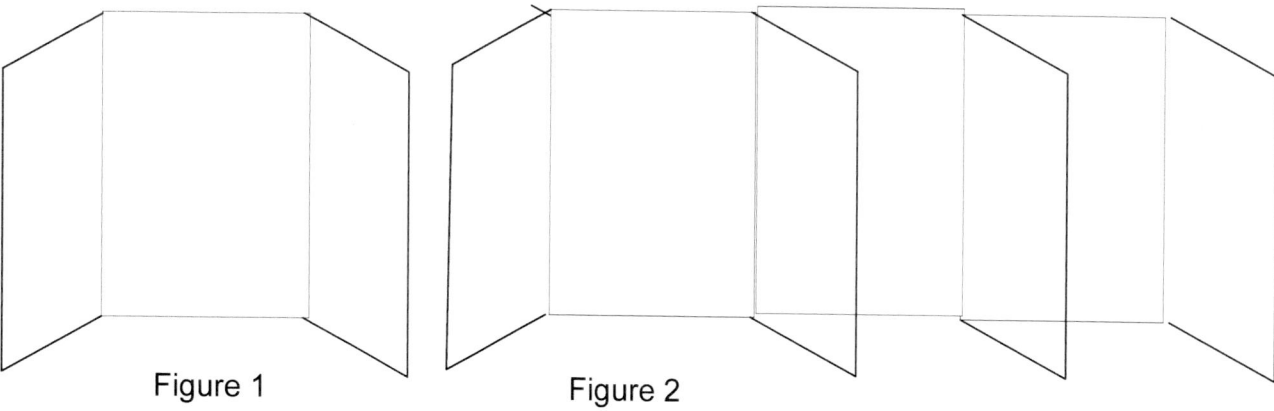

Figure 1   Figure 2

This is the "Layout" for your lapbook. The shapes are not exact on the layout, but you will get the idea of where each booklet should go inside your lapbook.

Inside of 1st Folder:

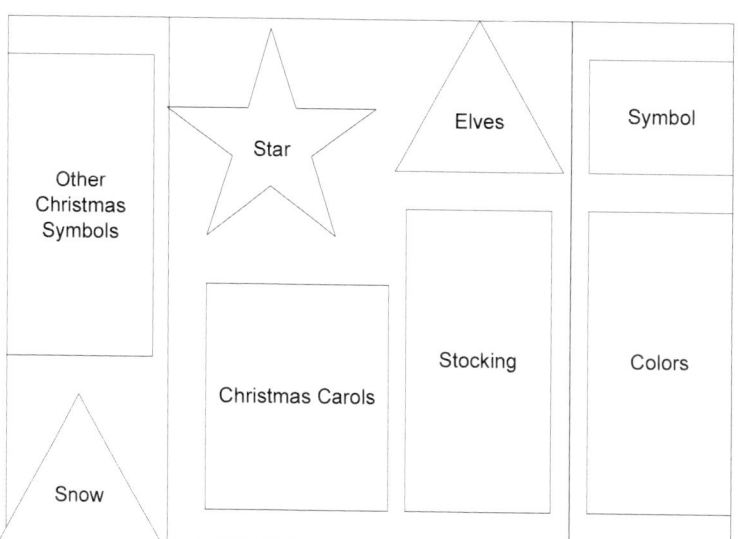

Continue ON........ ➡

Inside of 2nd Folder:

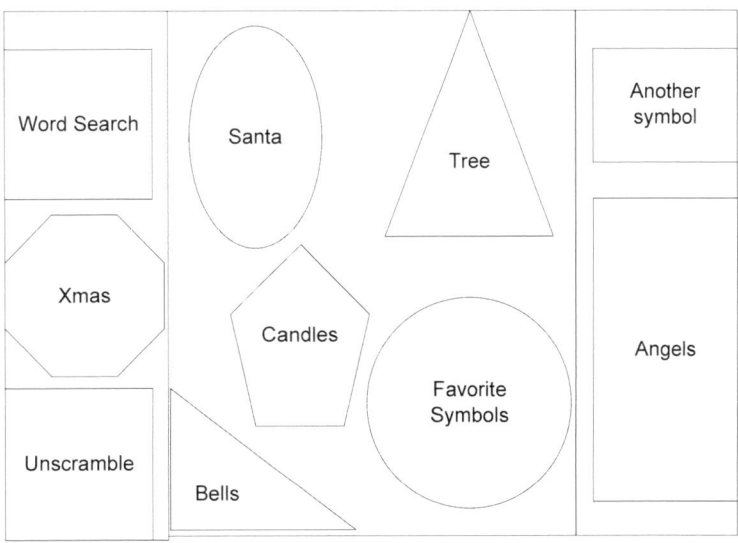

Inside of 3rd Folder:

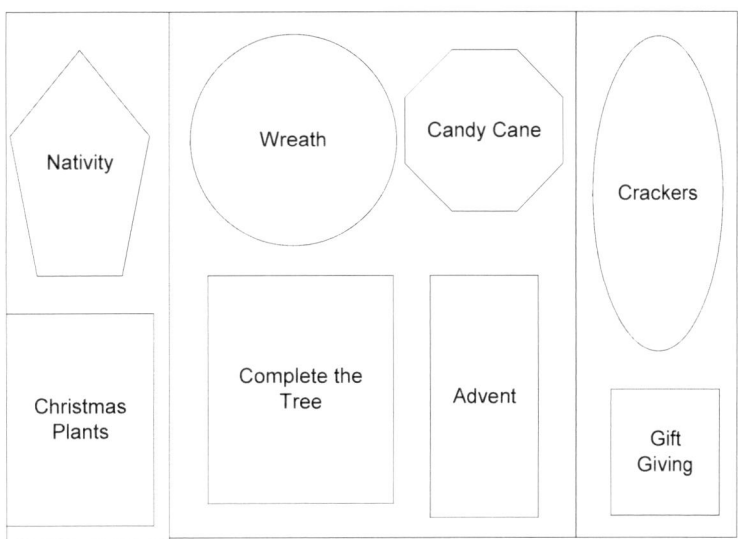

Christmas Symbols Lapbook
Lapbook Assembly Guide

Inside of 1st Folder:

1. Other Christmas Symbols Booklet: Cut out along the outer black line edges. Then fold along the center line, so that the words are on the front. Now, cut along the red dashed lines, so that you create little "flaps" that you can lift to write the information behind them.
2. Snow Booklet: Cut out along outer black line edges. Then, fold along center line so that title page is on front.
3. Star Booklet: Cut out along outer black line edges of each star. Place the one with the title on the top, and then punch a small hole in the top point. You may secure with a metal brad fastener or with a yellow ribbon.
4. Christmas Carols Booklet: Cut out around the black line edges of the booklet. Then fold along the center line, so that the picture and words are on the front.
5. Elves Booklet: Cut out along outer black line edge, and fold along center line, so that title is on front.
6. Stocking: Cut out along outer black line edge of the stocking shape. Then, mount it to a piece of colored paper before gluing into your folder.
7. What does "symbol" mean Booklet: Cut out along outer black line edge, and fold along center line, so that title is on front.
8. Colors of Christmas Booklet: Cut out around the outer black line edges of the booklet. Then, fold into thirds, with both ends folding toward the center. Make sure that the title is on the front. Now, cut along the lines between the color names. This will create little flaps to write your information under (a lot like the 1st booklet in this folder).

Inside of 2nd Folder:

1. Word Search Booklet: Cut out along the outer black line edges. Then, mount onto a slightly larger piece of paper of a different color, creating a small border around the edges. Then fold in the center, along an imaginary horizontal line, so that the word search is hidden inside. Only one side of the word search will be glued to the folder.
2. Xmas Booklet: Cut out along outer black line edges. Then, fold along each end toward the middle, so that title page is on front.
3. Unscramble Activity: Cut out along the outer black line edges. Then, mount onto a slightly larger piece of paper of a different color, creating a small border around the edges.
4. Santa Booklet: Cut out Santa. You don't have to cut every detail of his beard. Just cut a sort of "oval" shape around his beard. Then, cut out the 4 odd-shaped pieces that are on that page. These pieces should all be stacked on top of each other and then placed behind Santa's beard, so that all touch at the end of his beard. Then, put a staple through the dark line at the top of his beard, below his mouth and above the title box. You should now have a Santa with several pages to his beard. Now, mount this to a colored piece of paper, and then cut around it, leaving a small border. Take a piece of cotton from a cotton ball and tear it into a few pieces. Glue some on his eyebrows, some on his mustache, and some on the ball of his hat.

5. Candles Booklet: Cut out along outer black line edges. Then, fold along center line so that title page is on front.
6. Tree Booklet: Cut out along outer black line edges of each tree shape. Place the one with the title on the top, and then punch a small hole in the top point. There are a star and several ornaments on another page. Cut these out also. Punch a small hole through the star, and then secure it to the tree, through the holes you have already made in them. Use a metal brad fastener. Glue the ornaments on the tree in different places.
7. Bells Booklet: Cut out around the black line edges of the booklet. Then fold along the center line, so that the picture and words are on the front.
8. My Favorite Christmas Symbols Booklet: Cut out along outer black line edges of both circles. Cut out the portion of the title circle that says "cut out." Punch a small hole through the center of both circles. Secure them together with a metal brad fastener.
9. Angels Booklet: Cut out along outer black line edges of the booklet. Fold along the center line, so that the title and picture are on the front.
10. Another Symbol Booklet: Cut out along outer black line edge, and fold along center line, so that title is on front.

Inside of 3rd Folder:

1. Nativity Booklet: Cut out along the outer black line edges. Place the title page on top, and punch 2 small holes in the bottom of the pages. Secure together with a piece of straw or raffia.
2. Christmas Plants Booklet: Cut out along outer black line edges. Then, fold along center horizontal line so that the SPLIT title page is on the outside. Now, cut along the lines between the names of the plants, so that you are creating flaps that you can lift to write the information. Now, lay the booklet down on the table in front of you, so that the SPLIT title page is on the bottom. Fold the SPLIT title page over to the top...from each end, so that it now meets in the middle to create the words "Christmas Plants." You will now be able to see the completed words "Christmas Plants," which will have a split down the middle of them, and when you open up the booklet, you will see your 3 flaps that you cut.
3. Wreath Booklet: Cut out along outer black line edges of each circle. Place the one with the title on the top, and then punch a small hole through the center of the bow. You may secure with a red ribbon.
4. Candy Cane Booklet: Cut out around the black line edges of the booklet. Then fold along the center line, so that the picture and words are on the front.
5. Complete the Christmas Tree Activity: Cut out along outer black line edge. Then, glue to a slightly larger piece of paper of a different color, to create a small border.
6. Advent Booklet: Cut out along outer black line edges of the booklet. Then, fold along the center line, so that the title page is on the front.
7. Crackers Booklet: Cut out along outer black line edges of both pieces. Then, put the title page on top, and secure with a ribbon or yarn around one of the "twisted" areas.
8. Gift Giving Booklet: Cut out around the outer black line edges of the booklet. Then fold along the center line, so that the title/picture are on top.

Christmas Symbols Lapbook
Student Instructions

Cover:

The cover of your lapbook has purposely been left blank so that you may decorate it in any style you choose. Here are a few suggestions:

1. Go to www.enchantedlearning.com, and print out pictures of holiday items.
2. Cover the front with red or green paper, and draw ornaments.
3. Draw a picture of some of the people or places you learned about during your study.
4. Use your search engine to find coloring pages or clip art that tell about your study.
5. Use stickers to decorate.
6. Go to www.makingfriends.com, and print out a paper doll.
7. Go to http://www.dltk-kids.com/world/index.htm and print out coloring sheets or crafts to use on the cover or various places within your lapbook.

There are many websites listed within this Instruction Packet, all with permission. You may use those or use your own search engine to find information to fill your lapbook booklets. Two web sites which are very helpful are www.enchantedlearning.com and www.infoplease.com. Other useful websites, used with permission include the following: http://www.geocities.com/alexstevenson.geo/christmas, http://www.e-wreath.com/wreathhistory.html, http://www.athomeschool.com/unitstudy/christmas_symbols_05.htm, www.santas.net, www.northpole.com, www.lil-fingers.com, and others. The Internet Public Library Kids section also has a lot of useful information: http://www.ipl.org/div/kidspace.

Other Christmas Symbols Booklet:

Lift each flap to reveal a space for writing. Tell what you have learned about these symbols: Cards, Reindeer, and the Christmas Rose. You may choose to allow younger students to draw or paste pictures.

Snow Booklet:

Why is snow always associated with Christmas? It has a special meaning! Tell about it here.

Star Booklet:

Why is a star something that we always see at Christmas? Why is a star used on the top of Christmas trees? Tell about this symbol here.

Christmas Carols Booklet:

Why do we sing Christmas Carols? How did this tradition begin? If you have the black & white version, color the picture on the front of the booklet. You may also want to write the words to your favorite Christmas Carol.

Elves Booklet:

Write about the elves that we always read about at Christmas time. Also, color the picture on the front.

Stocking Booklet:

Do you know why we hang stockings at Christmas time? Write about this in the box on the stocking. Also, decorate this stocking. You may use cotton, glitter, crayons, whatever you choose.

What Does "Symbol" Mean Booklet:

Look up the definition of the word "symbol" and write it here.

Colors of Christmas Booklet:

Did you know that the colors of Christmas are also symbols? There is a special reason that each one is used at Christmas time. Tell about each one here. For an added touch, you might want to shade that section in that color!

Word Search Booklet:

Most of the symbols within this lapbook are hidden in this this word search! Can you find them? They go every direction, including backwards!! Good luck!

Xmas Booklet:

Have you ever seen the word Christmas written with an X in it? Do you know why? Write it here.

Unscramble Activity:

There are 5 of our symbols in this activity, but the letters are scrambled. Can you unscramble them?

Santa or St. Nick Booklet:

Where did the idea of Santa Claus come from? Ever heard of St. Nick? If you have the black & white version, color Santa, and decorate him. Write about this symbol on the pages of his beard.

Candles Booklet:

Do you often see a lot of candles at Christmas time? Tell about this symbol and color the ones on the front cover of the booklet (black & white version).

Bells Booklet:

Bells have a beautiful sound, but why do we see and hear them a lot at Christmas time? Tell about this symbol and color the ones on the front cover of the booklet (black & white version).

Christmas Tree & Ornaments Booklet:

Why do we put up Christmas trees and hang ornaments on them? Yes, those are symbols too! Put the star on this tree. Color the ornaments, and glue them all around the tree on the front of the cover. Then, tell about this symbols on the inside pages.

My Favorite Christmas Symbols Boolet:

There are so many symbols associated with this season. Which ones are your favorite ones? Write them inside this spinning wheel.

Another Christmas Symbol Booklet:

Can you think of other Christmas symbols that we didn't list in this lapbook? How about yule logs? Rudolph? The North Pole? Special foods we eat? Ribbon? Bows? Other traditions? Tell about one (or more) here.

Angels Booklet:

We hear about angels all the time, but especially around Christmas. Why is this? Also, color or decorate the angel on the front of the booklet. You may want to draw or glue pictures inside, or write words from a poem or scripture about angels.

Nativity Booklet:

We always see The Nativity Scene at Christmas. Many do not know why. Explain that here, and color the picture.

Christmas Plants Booklet:

What plants do you always see at Christmas? Poinsettia? Mistletoe? Holly? Open each flap, and tell about these symbols. If you have the black & white version, color them also.

Wreath Booklet:

At many times during the year, we see wreaths. However, they are abundant at Christmas time. Why is that? Tell about the special meaning. If you have the black & white version, decorate your wreath. You may use colors, glitter, colored rice, or anything you want.

Candy Cane Booklet:

Do you like to eat candy canes? Do you like to hang them on your tree? There are many stories about where candy canes actually originated. Write about one of them here.

Complete the Christmas Tree Activity:

Using the grid, draw the other side of this decorated Christmas tree. If you draw one square at a time, yours will look exactly like the other side! Then, have fun decorating it!

Advent Booklet:

Have you heard of Advent? Advent Wreaths? Advent Calendars? Tell about the symbols of Advent here.

Christmas Crackers Booklet:

Have you ever received or made a Christmas Cracker? Where did this tradition/symbol originate? Tell about it inside, and then decorate your Cracker!

Gift Giving Booklet:

Why do we give gifts at Christmas time? Explain this symbol here. If you have the black & white version, decorate your gift box.

Teacher's Guide
Christmas Symbols Lapbook

Christmas Trees

There are many legends involving the use of a tree in celebrating Christmas, and most of them come from Germany. The first involves St. Boniface, a missionary to Germany during the 8th century. According to legend, St. Boniface saw some people who were going to sacrifice a child to one of their gods, who was symbolized by an oak tree. To save the child's life, the saint cut down the oak tree with an ax, and a fir tree sprang from its stump! St. Boniface told the surprised people that the fir tree represented eternal life in Jesus. He also used the three points of the tree—a triangle—as a symbol for the Trinity of God the Father, God the Son and God the Holy Spirit.

Another legend involves Martin Luther, a German priest in the 16th century. The story says that he was walking home from a Christmas Eve service. Whether he saw stars shining through the evergreen trees or stars reflected off the icicles, the lights reminded him of Jesus, the Light of the World. The legend says he cut a small tree to take home, placing candles on its branches to replicate his experience.

Two centuries later, Queen Victoria's husband Prince Albert, a German, is credited with introducing the custom of Christmas trees to England at Windsor Castle. His trees were placed atop tables, despite being eight feet tall, and decorated with candles, candied fruits, gingerbread and eggs filled with sweetmeats. An angel figurine with outstretched wings topped each tree.

Other stories about the Christmas tree say it was used as a prop in a medieval play about Adam and Eve, which referred to it as the "Paradise Tree." Since apple trees no longer had their leaves or fruit on December 24, when the play was annually performed, an evergreen tree was hung with apples and used instead. In the 1800s, the Reform Church (now Lutheran Church), decorated evergreen trees as a reference to both the cross and everlasting life. Roses adorned the trees to represent the Rose of Sharon, and a single candle at the top stood for Jesus, the Light of the World.

As for the modern Christmas tree, it dates back to the 16th century Germany, when decorations of paper roses, apples, and wafers (to symbolize communion) adorned evergreen trees in homes throughout the country. Candles, candies, and confections were also used to extensively decorate trees prior to the decorations that can be found on store shelves today. A star or angel was put on top of the tree to symbolize what was found in the sky the night Jesus was born. Legend tells us that a poor family was unable to afford decorations for the Christmas tree, so spiders wove webs all over it during the night. Then, according to other traditions, either the rising sun or baby Jesus turned the webs into silver, which is why we use tinsel to decorate Christmas trees.

Glass bulb ornaments were first developed over 150 years ago by a German glass blower to replace heavier ornaments in Lauscha, Germany. Throughout the years, most families in the village became involved in making the shiny blown-glass balls. These ornaments first reached America in 1860, where they were sold on street corners in German communities before being popularized by F.W. Woolworth in his chain of stores. Companies in other countries began to copy them, with Corning Glass eventually mass-producing the glass ornaments by machines.

The 17th century German immigrants brought the Christmas trees traditions to America. The first outdoor tree in a public location was introduced in Finland in 1906. Electric candles lighted it. The first public tree in the United States followed in 1912.

Another legend of the evergreen tree says it was not always the tree we know it as today. According to the story, before the birth of Jesus, evergreen trees lost their leaves each winter, the same as other trees. However, when Mary, Joseph and Jesus were fleeing King Herod into Egypt, they had to hide in a group of cedar trees. To better hide the family, the legend says the trees grew green needles, and the white berries of the cedars turned blue to blend with Mary's blue robe. A related legend tells us that Jesus left his handprint in the fruit of the pine tree that hid the family from Herod's men. If you cut open a pinecone lengthwise, you can see the imprint of the tiny hand.

Commercial Christmas tree farming started in 1901, making it possible for those who don't live close to a forest to have a tree for the holiday. Some people will take their live tree and plant it in their yard after Christmas, saving the trees and beautifying their landscape.

Wreaths

Wreaths can be found in cultures throughout history. The champions of the Greek Olympic Games in 776BC were crowned with laurel wreaths. In ancient cultures, Eastern monarchs wore diadems, or fabric headbands adorned with jewels, as a sign of royalty. Eventually they transitioned to wall decoration, probably to showcase as a souvenir. One legend states that Christ's crown of thorns was actually made of holly with white berries. The story says that when the crown was put on his head, Jesus' blood turned the berries red. Before Jesus was born, Germans gathered evergreen wreaths, which 16th century Christians used to symbolize the hope and everlasting life in Christ.

One legend tells of a poor boy that had no gift to give to baby Jesus, so he made a tiny crown of leaves from a holly bush. When the little shepherd boy presented the crown, he began to cry when he saw the expensive gifts the others had given. According to the legend, when the baby touched the holly crown, the teardrops turned into scarlet berries and the leaves started gleaming.

In modern times, the wreath on a door means "welcome." The fact that wreaths are circular symbolizes everlasting life, the circle of family and God's unending love. The reason for evergreen wreaths at Christmas is to symbolize eternal life in Jesus Christ.

One of the more beautiful uses of the wreath symbol is the Advent wreath, which is thought to be inspired by the Swedish Crown of Lights, a crown adorned with candles worn by young girls on St. Lucia's Day.

Advent is the name for the four weeks before Christmas Day, which is a time of preparation for the celebration of Jesus' birth. It comes from the Latin "adventus," which means "to come." This season is a reminder to Christians of God's promise in the Old Testament that he would send a savior and of Jesus' New Testament promise that He will come again. Advent is a time for the church to focus on the events leading up to the birth of Christ.

The Advent wreath is made up of four candles attached around the outside of an evergreen wreath. The colors of the candles have meaning. Purple or blue candles symbolize royalty. A pink candle is used as the shepherd's candle or to stand for joy. There may also be a white candle in the center.

Each of the four Sundays before Christmas, a candle is lighted on the wreath, in order. The pink candle, if there is one, is usually the third one lit.

What do the candles mean? There are different traditions to explain their meanings. One has the candles labeled as the Prophet's candle, the Bethlehem candle, the Shepherd's candle and the Angel's candle, to represent sources of Good News about the coming of Jesus. The candles may also represent hope, love, joy and peace.

Mistletoe

One of the most well known Christmas plants is mistletoe. You may not know that it is a hemi parasitic plant, meaning it typically grows on the branches or trunk of a tree, sending roots into the tree to take up nutrients for its own growth. This is how mistletoe is most commonly found, though it is able to produce its own food through photosynthesis. The mistletoe that is most commonly used as a Christmas decoration (Phoradendron flavescens) is native to North America, growing all along the east coast as a parasite on trees. The other type (Viscum album) comes from Europe and is a green shrub with small, yellow flowers and sticky, poisonous white berries. This variety of mistletoe was commonly found on apple trees but only rarely on oak trees.

It was this oak variety of Viscum album mistletoe that was a sacred symbol of eternal life to ancient druids. It was hung over doorways to bring health, happiness and good luck as it warded off evil from the home. This mistletoe was also considered to be a magical plant in many early European traditions—giving life and fertility, protecting against poison, extinguishing fires, bringing luck to recipients, and providing miraculous healing.

The name "mistletoe" has its origins in the ancient belief that the plant sprang from bird droppings, which was related to the belief that life could spontaneously spring out of dung. Mistletoe often appeared on a branch where a bird had left droppings. The Anglo-Saxon word "mistel" means "dung," and "tan" is their word for "twig," which translates to "dung on a twig." The scientific explanation of 16th century botanist revealed that birds passed the mistletoe plant seeds through their digestive tracts, leaving them behind in their droppings. Additionally, it was observed that the sticky berry seeds of mistletoe clung to the bills of birds; the seeds were scattered when birds rubbed their bills on branches to clean their bills.

When many people today hear the word "mistletoe," images of couple kissing under it come to mind. This tradition is first associated with the Greek festival of Saturnalia and later marriage rituals. It was considered a plant of peace in Scandinavia; enemies could declare a true under it or fighting spouses could "kiss and make up" beneath its berries. One tradition says the Scandinavian goddess Frigga's son Balder was shot with an arrow made of mistletoe. Her tears saved Balder, and she ordered mistletoe should not be used to harm others again. The goddess is said to have made the plant a symbol of love instead, kissing anyone standing under it. It was also considered a symbol of peace to the Romans, who kissed under the hanging plant.

Balls of greens and berries were placed in doorways as a way for a young man to surprise a female with a kiss. In 18th century England, mistletoe was tied to the bottoms of the balls and thus the kissing tradition began. The Christmas mistletoe is burned on the twelfth night in some parts of England to keep the boys and girls who kissed under it from marrying each other. Another tradition says that a man should pluck a berry from the mistletoe when he kisses a woman under the plant; when the last berry is gone, kissing should cease!

Modern Christian symbolism for mistletoe is that it represents eternal life, since it is perennially green. It is also seen as a symbol of peace.

Other Christmas Plants

With its beautiful red and green, the poinsettia is thought of as a Christmas plant. The plant was named after Joel Poinsett, a South Carolina native serving as an ambassador to Mexico when he discovered the plant. In the 1800s, he sent some of the flowers home, where they did well in his greenhouse.

Mexican legend says a poor child was on his way to church on Christmas Eve, but had no gift to give the Christ child, so he gathered a small bouquet of weeds. Laid at the feet of the baby, the weeds miraculously transformed into the bright red and white leaves of a poinsettia plant. One variation of this legend says the poor child kneeled at the altar, praying for a gift to present to the Christ child. Suddenly a plant grew at his feet, known as The Flower of the Holy Night, which later became called the poinsettia.

An unrelated legend about the poinsettia tells of the plant's origins and meaning: The Star of Bethlehem shone on the earth, which responded by producing a plant to resemble the star's beauty. The flower of the new plant was star-shaped, with white petals and a golden star center. The legend says the flower changed yet again when Jesus died on the cross, turning its white petals red in remembrance of Jesus' blood. To honor the purity of Jesus' sacrifice, other poinsettias remained white.

Modern Christian symbolism says poinsettias remind us that Jesus will meet all of our needs.

The evergreen leaves of holly led the ancient druids to consider it sacred. They brought it indoors during winter months to shelter the spirits who inhabited the plant. Holly was believed to ward off evil spirits, as well as bad weather, by the Teutonic people, who placed it around their homes. Northern Europeans considered it to be a good-luck charm, tying it to bedposts to guard against the demons and ghosts whose voices could be heard in winter winds.

An English tradition declares the two types of holly as male (with prickles on its leaves) and female (smooth leaves). The first type of holly brought into the house foretells who will rule the household for that year. Therefore, both types of holly were often brought into a home at the same time to avoid a fight.

Modern Christian symbolism uses prickly holly leaves to remind us of the crown of thorns Jesus wore on his head. The red berries are said to be a reminder of the blood Jesus shed on the cross. The perennial green leaves represent eternal life. Since holly berries can come in different colors, the green berries are said to represent the cross of wood, white berries to represent Jesus' purity, and black berries to represent Jesus' death.

Ivy is always green and is seen as a symbol of eternal life. It is used for decorating at Christmastime.

Rosemary has some legends about it, both which refer to the Nativity. According to one, Mary's blue cloak gave the herb its color. When Mary and Joseph were fleeing Bethlehem for Egypt with young Jesus, Mary is said to have laid her cloak on a rosemary bush with white flowers. The blue of her cloak turned the rosemary blue. Another legend has Mary washing her child's clothes in a stream while fleeing to Egypt. She laid them on a rosemary bush to dry. On account of the humble service the rosemary gave to the Savior, the plant became blue. According to tradition, the humble rosemary plant will never grow higher than Jesus was tall; if it outlives Jesus' 33 years, the plant will not grow taller, just wider.

The legend of the Christmas Rose is like that of the poinsettia, in that it is about a poor child wanting to give a gift to baby Jesus. According to the story, when Jesus was young, Wise Men came from the East, bearing gifts of gold, frankincense and myrrh. In the field, a young shepherdess cried because she had no gift to offer the child. It is said that flowers sprang up where her tears fell. She gathered them and took them to Jesus. In adoration for her Savior, the girl knelt at the crib so Jesus could see the flowers. His hands touched the petals in a few places and a delicate pink appeared! Thus began the new flower, the Christmas Rose, which blooms more abundantly at Christmas than any other time of year.

The 12 Days of Christmas

Did you know that in the church, "Christmas" can mean "Christmastide," which includes Christmas Day, as well as the days after? That is where the "twelve days of Christmas" comes from! During the Middle Ages, Christmas was extended from a one-day holiday to a 12-day celebration. Many Christians celebrate through January 6, which is the Epiphany, a feast day celebrating the revelation of God the Son as the human being in Jesus Christ. This date is also called the 12th Day of Christmas, the Twelfth Night, Three Kings' Day and the Theophany.

According to legend, the Roman Catholics made up a song to teach their faith to their children during a time when it was illegal to be a Catholic (though the song was first published in England in 1780). In 1982, Father Hal Stockert claims to have found references to the hidden meaning in the song in letters written by a priest in Ireland.

Using symbols to represent parts of the faith, the song's subject is "my true love" which refers to God. "Me" stands for the baptized believers (or Christians), and "the partridge in a pear tree" means Jesus, who was a gift from God.

The other symbols represent parts of the Christian faith:
- Two turtledoves stand for The Old Testament and New Testament of the Bible.
- Three French hens represent Faith, Hope and Charity, the Theological Virtues, otherwise known as "faith, hope and love," three gifts of the Spirit.
- Four calling birds are the Four Gospels and/or the Four Evangelists (Matthew, Mark, Luke and John), so called because they "sing" the song of salvation through Jesus Christ for all to hear.
- Five Golden Rings stand for the first five books of the Old Testament, known as the Pentateuch or the books of Moses, which gives the history of man's fall from grace.
- Six geese-a-laying refer to the six days of creation (Genesis 1).
- Seven swans-a-swimming are the seven gifts of the Holy Spirit, or the seven sacraments, which are ceremonies that point to what is sacred, significant and important for Christians (baptism, Eucharist/communion, reconciliation, confirmation, marriage, Holy orders/ordination of priests, and anointing of the sick).
- Eight maids-a-milking means the eight beatitudes, mentioned in Jesus' Sermon on the Mount (Matthew 5-7).
- Nine ladies dancing symbolized the nine Fruits of the Holy Spirit (love, joy, peace, patience, kindness, goodness, faithfulness, gentleness and self-control—Galatians 5:22-23).
- Ten lords-a-leaping represent the Ten Commandments (Exodus 20).
- Eleven pipers piping are the eleven faithful apostles.
- Twelve drummers drumming stand for the twelve points of doctrine in the Apostle's Creed.

Concrete historic evidence points to a game based on the song in medieval England and France. In this singing game, the first person sang a stanza of the song, followed by the second player who had to sing both the second stanza and the first stanza. This repeated until someone missed a stanza and had to pay some sort of penalty, usually decided before the game. Since there is proof that the game existed before the 16th century, there is a possibility that this common game was used to teach the Roman Catholics catechism.

Modern Christian symbolism uses the song to remind us that many Christians gave their lives for the faith (martyrs).

Santa Claus/St. Nicholas and Stockings

Santa Claus, Kris Kringle, Sinterklaas, Father Christmas, Saint Nicholas—these all refer to the same Christmas gift-giver, known throughout the world by many different names. There are many legends surrounding him.

Born in 280 AD, Nicholas was orphaned at a young age and became a Christian minister. Later, he was elected bishop in Asia Minor (now Turkey). He was known for his wisdom, charity, generosity, and compassion. One legend about him says Nicholas saved three daughters of a poor man from lives of prostitution by tossing bags of gold through a window of the family home; it is said that one of the bags landed in a stocking that had been hung up to dry, which is where the practice of Christmas stockings began. Another story tells that Nicholas would dress in disguise and give presents to the poor children in the streets. It is also said that he came from a wealthy family and gave all his money to the less fortunate. He later became known as St. Nicholas. To learn more about the real St. Nicholas, read *The Miracle of Saint Nicholas* by Gloria Whelan, *The Real Santa Claus* by Marianna Mayer, and *The Saint Nicholas Secret* by Dennis E. Engleman.

Around the world, many countries have developed their own versions of this gift-giving man. European stories claim he saved sailors from a storm, as well as giving gifts to the poor and defending children. Germans call him Sankt Nikolaus, and he is known as Sanct Herr Nicholass or Sinter Klass in Holland. Tradition from those countries has him riding through the sky on a horse, accompanied by Black Peter, who would whip the naughty children.

German Protestants began recognizing the Christ child as the giver of gifts with the name Christkindl, which evolved into Kris Kringle, another name for St. Nicholas. He is also known as Père Noel in France, Julenisse in Scandinavia, and Father Christmas in England.

In America, the legend of Santa Claus developed out of the Dutch traditions from the 17th and 18th centuries. Washington Irving wrote about the arrival of St. Nicholas on horseback in his comic *History of New York*, which also described the saint as a plump and jolly old man. In 1823 Clement Clarke Moore further redefined the gift-giving man in his famous poem, "A Visit from St. Nicholas," which is more commonly recognized as "The Night Before Christmas." It was this poem that gave Americans the names of his eight reindeer. The name change did not come about until the 1860s when cartoonist Thomas Nast drew a visual image of the saint and named him "Santa Claus." Then, in the 1920s, Santa was given a heavy mustache, crinkled eyes and more when artist Haddon Sundblom created a series of ads for Coca-Cola.

The tradition of elves helping Santa Claus most likely evolved from Scandinavian countries where the creatures were either helpful or mean-spirited. The nature of the elves depended on whether a person was "naughty" or "nice." Their purpose in helping Father Christmas came through Scandinavian writers in the mid-1800s.

Modern Christian symbolism reminds us that Saint Nicholas is a great example of how Christians should use their faith to help others, by giving to the poor or showing kindness and patience to the elderly and children.

Gift-giving at Christmas

The ancient Roman custom of gift giving at Saturnalia, a festival to honor the god Saturn, is where the exchanging of Christmas presents is first found. Christians then took this tradition and told that the custom related to the gifts of gold, frankincense and myrrh the Magi (wise men) had brought to Jesus from the East.

Modern Christian tradition says the presents represent God's gift to the world in Jesus, as well as the gifts He daily gives.

Bells

Mentioned in the Old Testament of the Bible as being used on the robes of high priests, bells have also become associated with Christmas throughout time. During the Middle Ages, bells were rung to warn the devil of the approaching birth of the Christ Child. Church bells announced the Midnight Mass. Pagan celebrations included the ringing of bells to drive out evil spirits.

Cards

The first person to give a Christmas card is thought to be Sir Henry Cole of England. He was the first director of London's Victoria and Albert Museum. Cole found himself too busy in the Christmas season to write individual Christmas letters to friends, so in 1843, he commissioned J.C. Horsley to design the first Christmas card. It was sold in London, and one thousand of these cards were produced.

Louis Prang, who set up nationwide contests to find the best designs to use on his cards, first printed American Christmas cards in 1875.

Themes on early cards were as varied as holiday traditions themselves. Home scenes, nature scenes and nativity themes were the most common.

Nutcrackers

A common and practical Christmas gift, nutcrackers were made even more famous after Tchaikovsky's famous ballet, *The Nutcracker*. These gifts could be made from a piece of scrap wood and were popular among the poor. The nutcrackers were usually dressed as soldiers or government officials, after the popular ballet. Modern Christian symbolism points to the German proverb, "God gives us the nuts, but we have to break them ourselves," a reminder that nothing in life should come without hard work.

Christmas Crackers

Said to be of French origin, Christmas crackers can be traced back to the mid-19th century. At first they were simply sweets enclosed in twists of colored paper. English pastry cook Tom Smith saw them on a trip to Paris and began copying the idea of the wrapper. He added other small gifts and slips of paper inscribed with jokes, advice and other sayings.

His idea did not catch on immediately. Then on Christmas Night 1846, Smith was sitting by the fireplace, listening to the crackling sound of the burning logs. He decided to imitate the sound by inserting a small explosive in the paper tube; pulling from either side of the tube would set it off with a bang, thus the cracker was named.

The Nativity

Christians celebrate Christmas Day as the birthday of Jesus. "Nativity" means "birth, especially the conditions of being born" and more specifically, when capitalized, it refers to the birth of Jesus. The Nativity scenes remembered at the holiday are drawn directly from the Bible. Mary, the mother of Jesus, and Joseph, her husband, are found in the scene, as are shepherds, angels and animals. The wise men are usually placed in the nativity as well, though they did not come to visit the family until Jesus was older (Matthew 2:1-12).

St. Francis of Assisi, who was well known for his love of animals, made the first Nativity scene in the 1200s with live animals and people. It was outside a cave in Greccio, Italy. Francis stood in front of the manger as crowds gathered to watch; he would first recite the Gospel related to the scene, followed by a sermon.

Sometimes the Nativity is called the crèche, which refers to the feeding trough or manger that the baby Jesus was laid in to sleep.

Star

Stars are often used to adorn the top of Christmas trees. The book of Matthew in the Bible mentions a star that the wise men followed from the east (2:1-2). Named the Star of Bethlehem, it was an astronomical phenomenon that made Jesus' birth known to those who watched the stars, such as the wise men. There are many theories regarding the star, from believing it was a supernova or comet, to thinking it was a conjunction of the planets. It most likely happened around 7BC, which was probably the birth year of Jesus.

Xmas

While some people use this shortened version of Christmas to make the holiday less religious, Xmas has its roots in Greek. The X is the formal representation of "chi," as in the initial of the name Christ. Additionally, the Greek work for Christ is "Xristos." Xmas became popular during the 1500s as a way to shorten Christmas.

Colors of Christmas

Reds and greens are used to symbolize Christmas because of the winter plants they represent (holly, mistletoe, poinsettias, evergreen trees). White is used to symbolize the snow on the ground during winter.

Modern Christian symbolism gives special meaning to the colors for believers:
- Red stands for Jesus' blood shed for our sin on the cross.
- Green stands for the eternal life believers have in Jesus.
- White reminds us of the purity of Christ.
- Gold stands for Christ the Divine (Rev. 3:18).
- Silver reminds us of the redemption for all in Jesus.

Candy Canes

Candy canes began as simply straight hard sugar sticks of white over 350 years ago. Then, in the 1670s the choirmaster of Cologne Cathedral in Germany bent the candy sticks into canes to represent a shepherd's staff.

There is a Christian legend regarding the modern candy cane. It says there was a candy maker in Indiana who wanted to invent a candy to be a witness to Christ. He used hard candy to symbolize that Jesus is the rock of ages, and shaped it so it could represent either a "J" for Jesus or a shepherd's staff. The white background of the candy symbolized the purity of Christ. Then the red was added—a large stripe to represent the blood Jesus shed on the cross, and three thin stripes to represent the lashes He received from the Roman soldiers. Occasionally, a green stripe is added to the candy cane as a reminder of the gift God gave the world in Jesus.

Also according to legend, the flavor of peppermint was used because is similar to the herb hyssop, which was used in Old Testament times for purification and sacrifice. Thus, the flavor of the candy even represents Jesus' sacrifice for the sins of the world.

Carols

At Christmastime you hear special music everywhere. These songs, called carols, usually have a religious or festive theme to them. Some even tell a story, and most were poems before they were put with music and made into Christmas carols.

Church music at this time was very somber. In contrast, the carols were lively tunes which some say expressed the joy singers felt about the birth of Jesus. This led to the songs being banned from church ceremonies for a time. Francis of Assisi (the man who started the live Nativity) was the first to bring the carols into a church service. It was during a Midnight Mass in a cave in Greccio in 1223.

Later, during the Middle Ages, carols were sung at holiday plays about the Nativity. Audience members would leave the show still singing the carols.

Angels

The Bible tells us that angels proclaimed the coming of the Messiah and announced His birth. God sent the angel Gabriel to Mary to tell her that she would be the mother of the Messiah and that she was to name Him Jesus (Luke 1:26-38).

Angels also appeared to the shepherds in the field, announcing the birth of Jesus (Luke 2:9-16).

Yule Log

The Yule log is a large wooden log burned in the hearth as part of Christmas celebrations. It was thought the Yule log is a magical source of fuel for the sun; it symbolized the sun's light, warmth and life-giving abilities. German pagans are thought to be the first to use this in their traditions. Later, the British adopted it, and Father Christmas was often shown in pictures carrying a Yule log. Christians adopted the practice of a Yule log, placing it on the hearth on Christmas Eve, where it would burn for at least 12 hours. There were strict rules regarding the Yule log, from how it was received (you could not buy one for yourself—it must be a gift), to how it is kindled and when the fire could go it (it must be put out, not go out by itself).

Why is Christmas in December?

The Bible does not give a birth date for Jesus; it simply says He was born at God's appointed time.

Ancient cultures recognized the shortest day of the year, the Winter Solstice—on or around December 22—and had festivals following it to bring the sun back. Romans even put candles in their windows for this purpose. Evergreen trees were a sign that the sun would come back, so Germanic people decorated them.

Many claim that the Roman Catholic Church chose the date of December 25 to take the place of an existing pagan holiday, and that is probably the case for St. Valentine's Day and All Saints Day. However, the Nativity is found on a list of Christian feasts before Constantine was emperor. Some believe this Christian observance was based on the Jewish custom of Chanukah, the festival of lights. Jesus is known as the Light of the World in the Bible, and this time of year is typically dark and cold (at least in the Northern Hemisphere).

Lights and Candles

As mentioned above, Pagan festivals during the dark days of winter used candles and fires to scare away darkness. Jesus came and was known as the Light of the World, and candles remind us of this truth. People throughout Europe still use candles in their windows and on their Christmas trees instead of lights.

During Advent (as previously mentioned), candles are used to remind us of the coming Light, when Jesus will return. In Swedish tradition, St. Lucia wears a crown of candles to celebrate her feast day, December 13.

There is also a legend of a Christmas candle, which demonstrates how Christians use candles to represent the peace and light that Jesus brings. A long time ago, an old cobbler and his wife lived in a little Austrian village. Though they were extremely poor, the couple shared their belongings with others. Each night they would place a lit candle in the cottage window; this was seen as a sign of hospitality to travelers in need of shelter. Despite hard times, through war and famine, the mysterious charm of the lit candle in the window—the sign of their generosity—guarded them and the couple suffered much less than their neighbors in the village.

On Christmas Eve, the villagers gathered to find a solution to the problems they were experiencing. Someone remembered that the cobbler and his wife seemed to be spared the hardships the others were facing. When it was remembered that the couple put a lit candle in the window, the villagers decided perhaps that was the couple's charm and to put a candle in each of their own windows.

The next morning, before sunrise, a messenger brought news of peace to the village. They choose to thank God for the blessing and vowed to light candles each Christmas Eve.

Snow

In the Northern Hemisphere, snow is related to Christmas as a matter of weather—since the holiday is in December, and there is likely to be snow in many places!

Snow is used as a symbol of purity because of its whiteness and freshness. In the Bible it is often mentioned with the washing away of sins (Ps. 51:7; Is. 1:18). Ancient people believed the sky was a dome with windows and doors, through which angels, snow and rain might descend as needed (Gen 7:11; Is. 24:18; Mal. 3:10). God is credited with the power to send snow to protect or hinder in battle (Job 37:6; Job 38:22-23).

Snowfall was a rare occurrence in Palestine, except on the high mountains. To Israelites, the snow appeared luminous because of the reflection of the sun's rays on these mountains. This led to the association of snow with heavenly beings and their garments (Dan. 7:9; Matt. 28:3, Mark 9:3).

Other December Holidays

Jewish tradition celebrates the festival of lights, known as Chanukah (also spelled Hanukkah). This is a celebration that predates the birth of Jesus. It is eight days long and commemorates the defeat of the Greeks by a small Jewish army. A menorah is a seven-branched candelabrum used in the Temple. The Temple was cleansed and rededicated after the defeat of the Greeks. The eternal flame was relit, but only one flask of the sacred oil for it remained. That should have only been enough to last one day, but the Israelites celebrated because a miracle caused it to last for lasted eight days.

Meaning "first fruits," Kwanzaa is an African-American cultural festival celebrated December 26 through January 1. There are seven principles observed during the festivities: unity, self-determination, collective work and responsibility, cooperative economics, purpose, creativity and faith.

Folder #1

Stocking

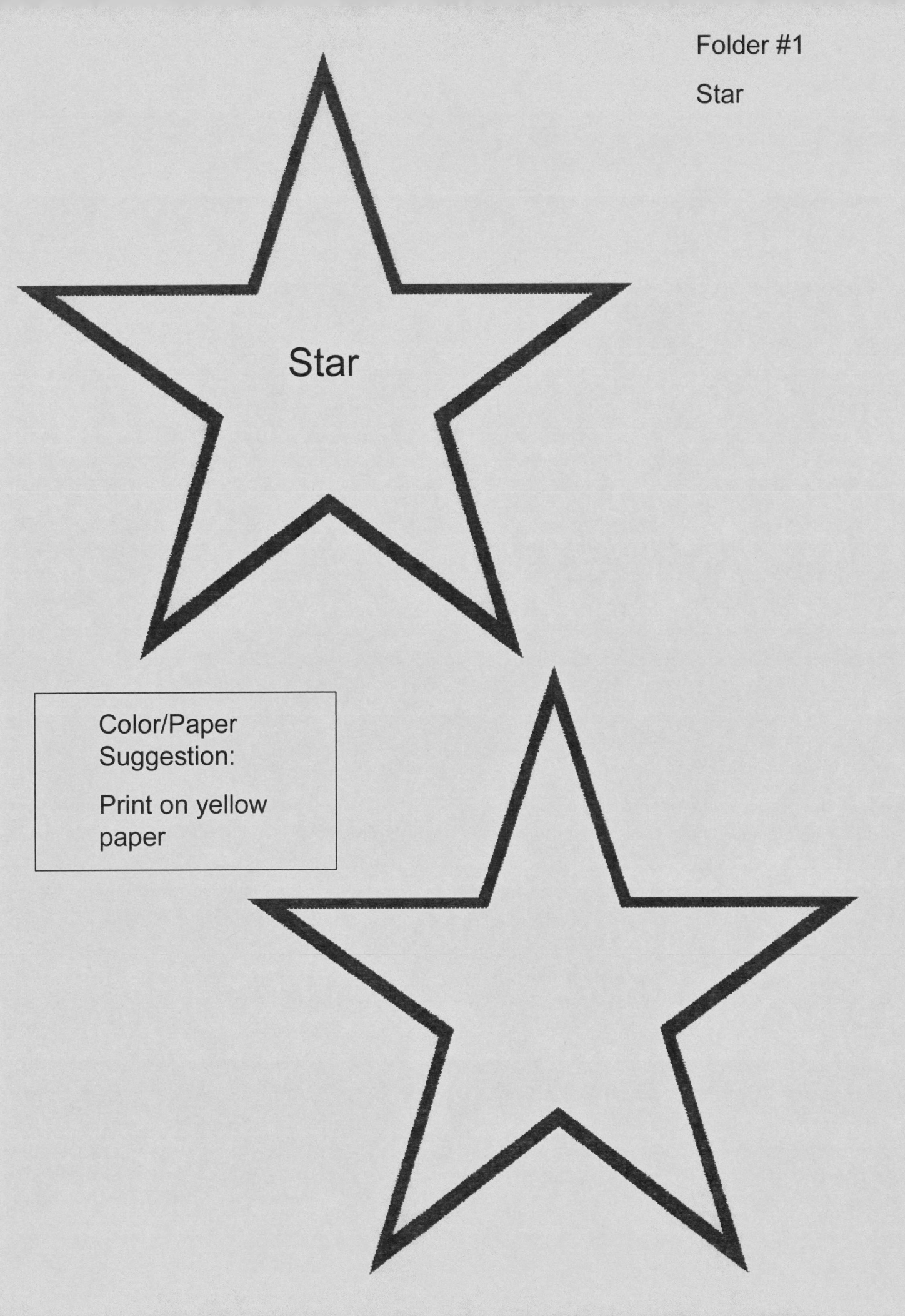

Folder #1

Carols

Folder #1

Colors of Christmas

Red

Green

The Colors Of Christmas

Silver

Gold

White

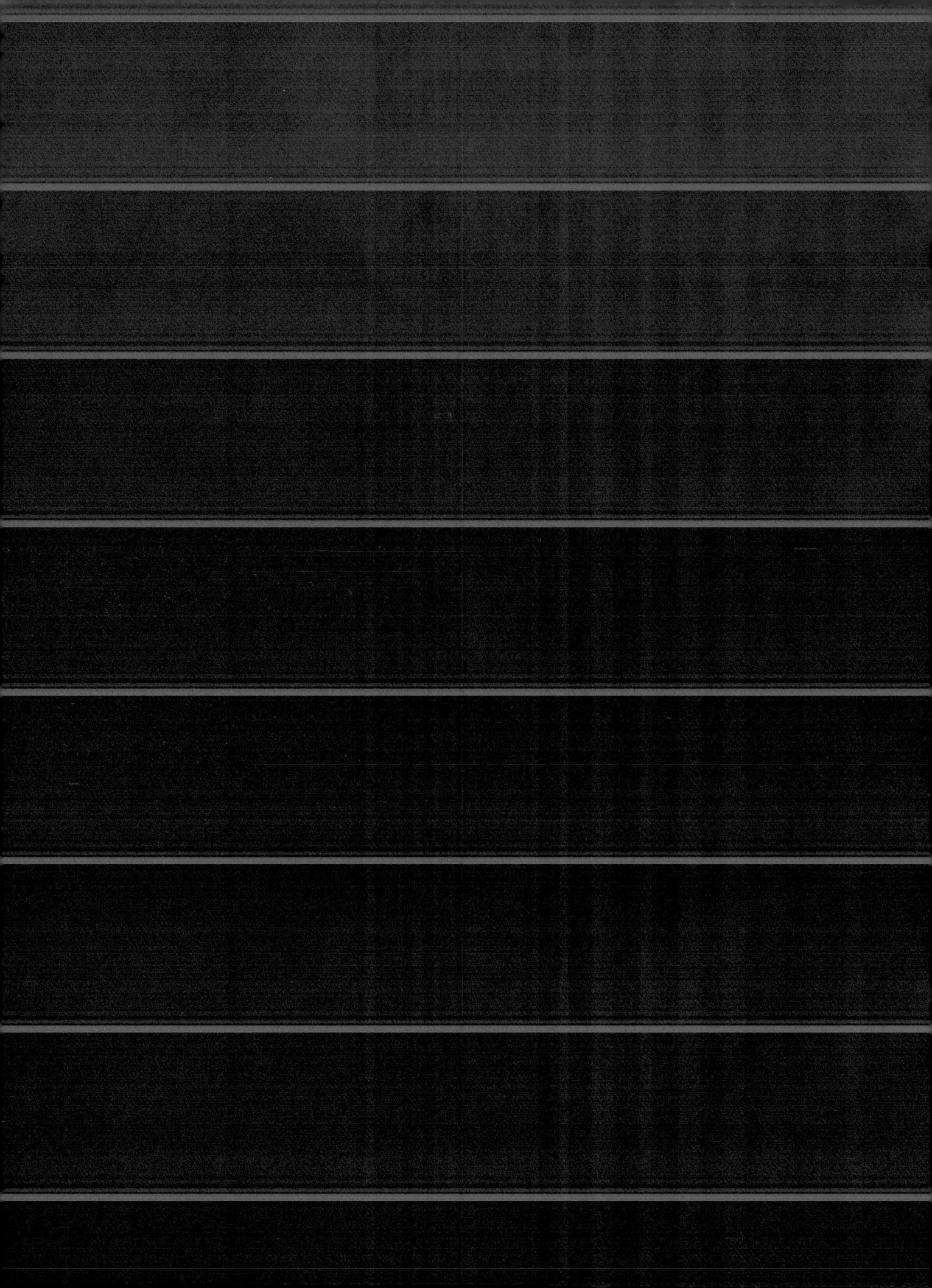

Folder #1

Elves

Folder #1

*Symbol

*Snow

What does the word "symbol" mean?

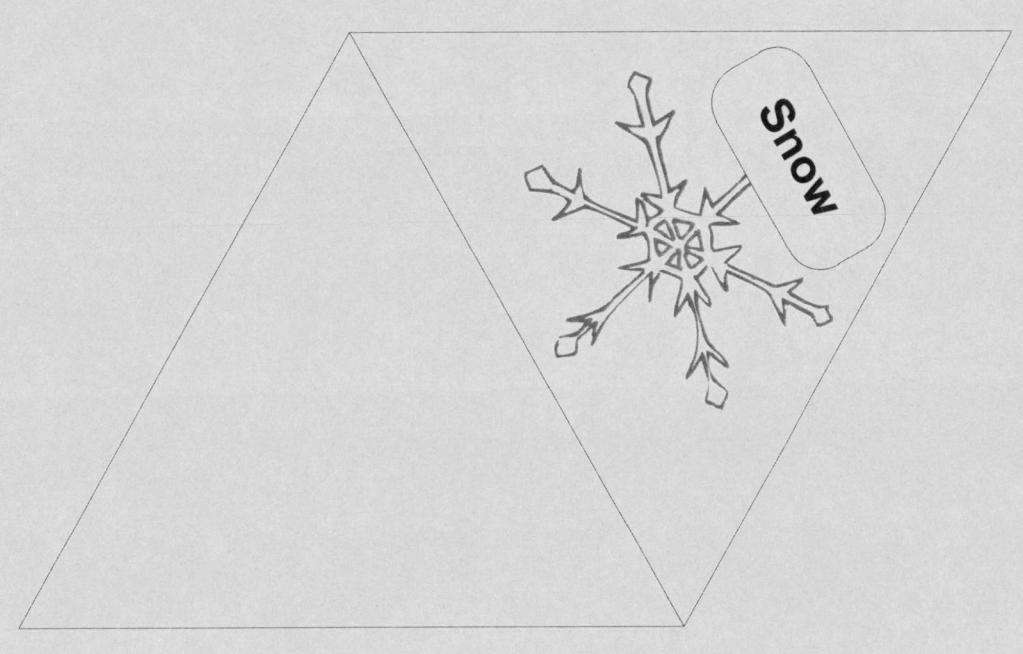

Folder #1

Other

OTHER CHRISTMAS SYMBOLS

Cards

Reindeer

Christmas Rose

Folder #2

Tree Booklet

The items on this page go with the Christmas trees on the next page.

Color/Paper Suggestion:

Print on white paper with colored ink.

Folder #2
Tree Booklet

Legends of the Christmas Tree, Ornaments, and Lights

Christmas Tree

Color/Paper Suggestion:

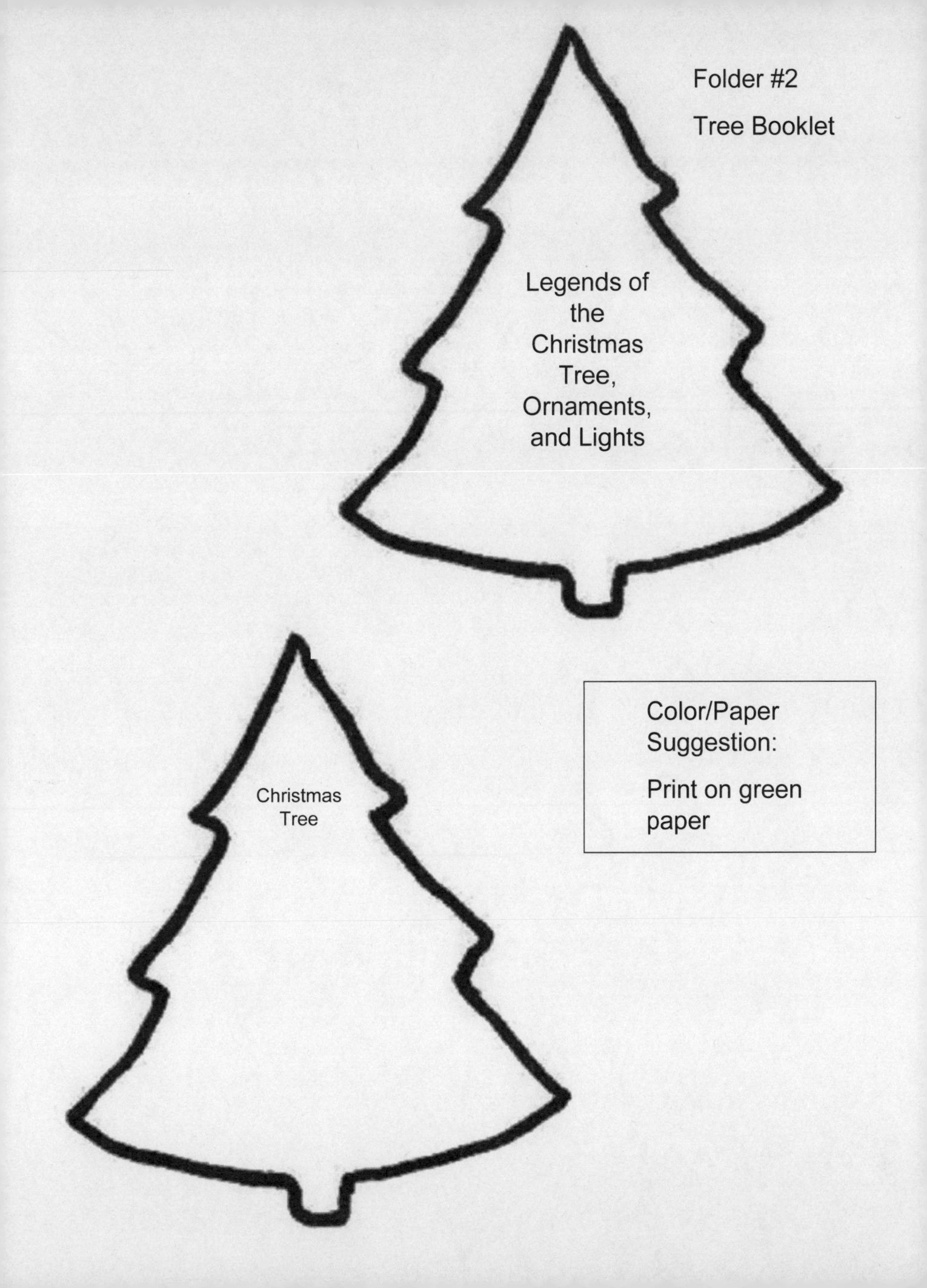

Print on green paper

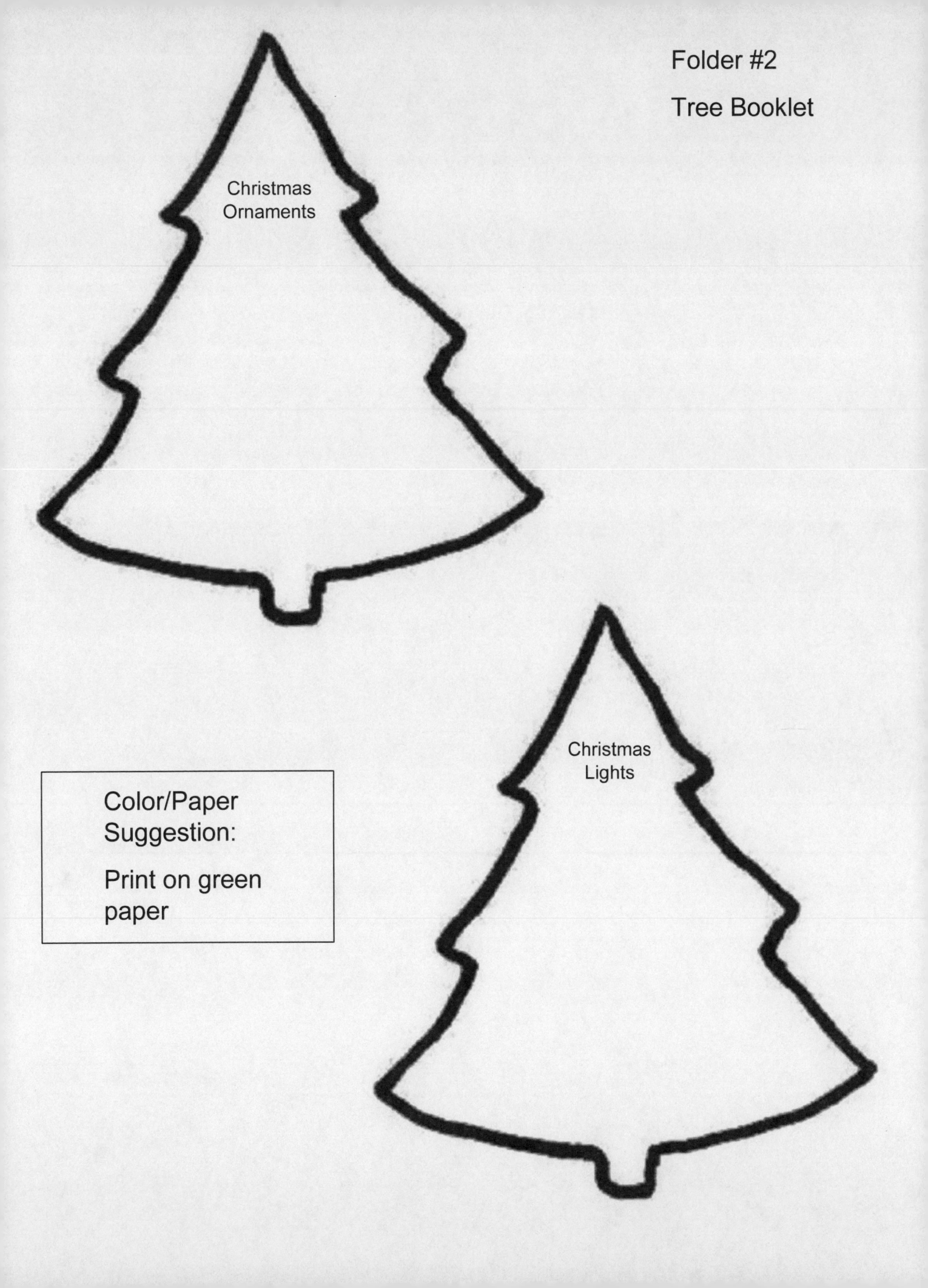

Folder #2

Tree Booklet

Christmas Ornaments

Christmas Lights

Color/Paper Suggestion:

Print on green paper

Folder #2

*Word Search

*Unscramble

CANDY CANE	CRACKER	SILVER	CARDS
WHITE	STAR	ROSE	CANDLE
GREEN	NATIVITY	SANTA	WREATH
BELL	ANGEL	ADVENT	REINDEER
ORNAMENT	GIFT	TREE	
GOLD	CAROL	XMAS	
ELF	RED	STOCKING	

```
Y T I V I T A N E N H W E E A
A A X R O S E C L E L R T R T
T N D N A C D H F E O A M L W
N H T A E R W R E R O A R E M
A D V A A T A L G G E T E G B
S N D C F T E N R N N L V N V
E W F I S T I E A E L N L A T
E C G N I K E C V E A I I L E
A A I H C D Y D B S H O S G N
G A W O N D A R E D C A R O L
O G T I N C D M E N T R E E N
L S E A R N D E C R A C K E R
D R C O R N A M E N T G C S B
S A M X A E L D N A C A R D S
M N N C D E C R A Y E L N T N
```

Unscramble these symbols:

llbe _____

dancles _____

tawreh _____

costgnik _____

tasna _____

Folder #2

Santa

Santa Claus
& St. Nick

Folder #2

*Bells

*Another Symbol

Bells

Do you know of another symbol of Christmas?

Color/Paper Suggestion:

Print on white paper with colored ink

Folder #2

Angels

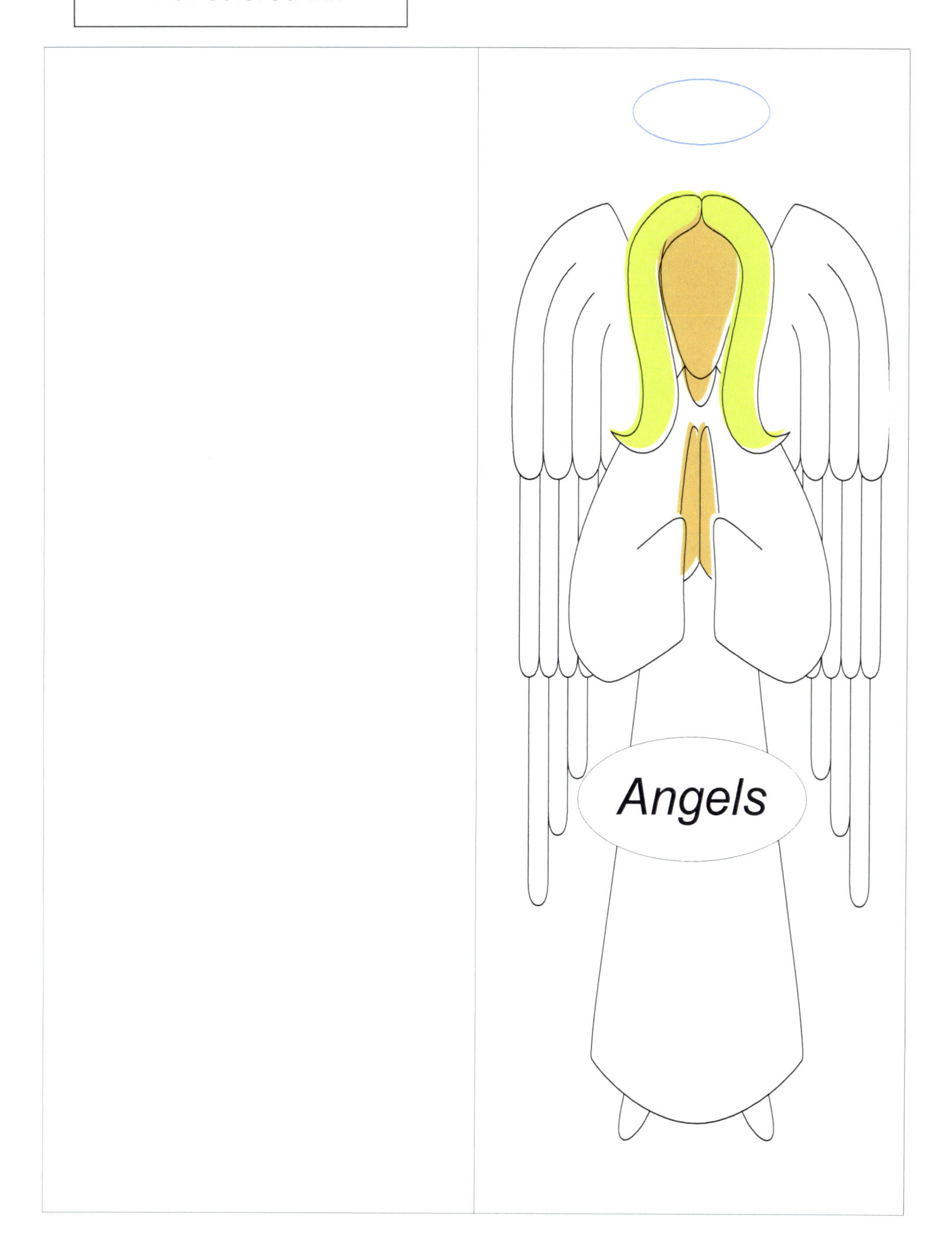

Angels

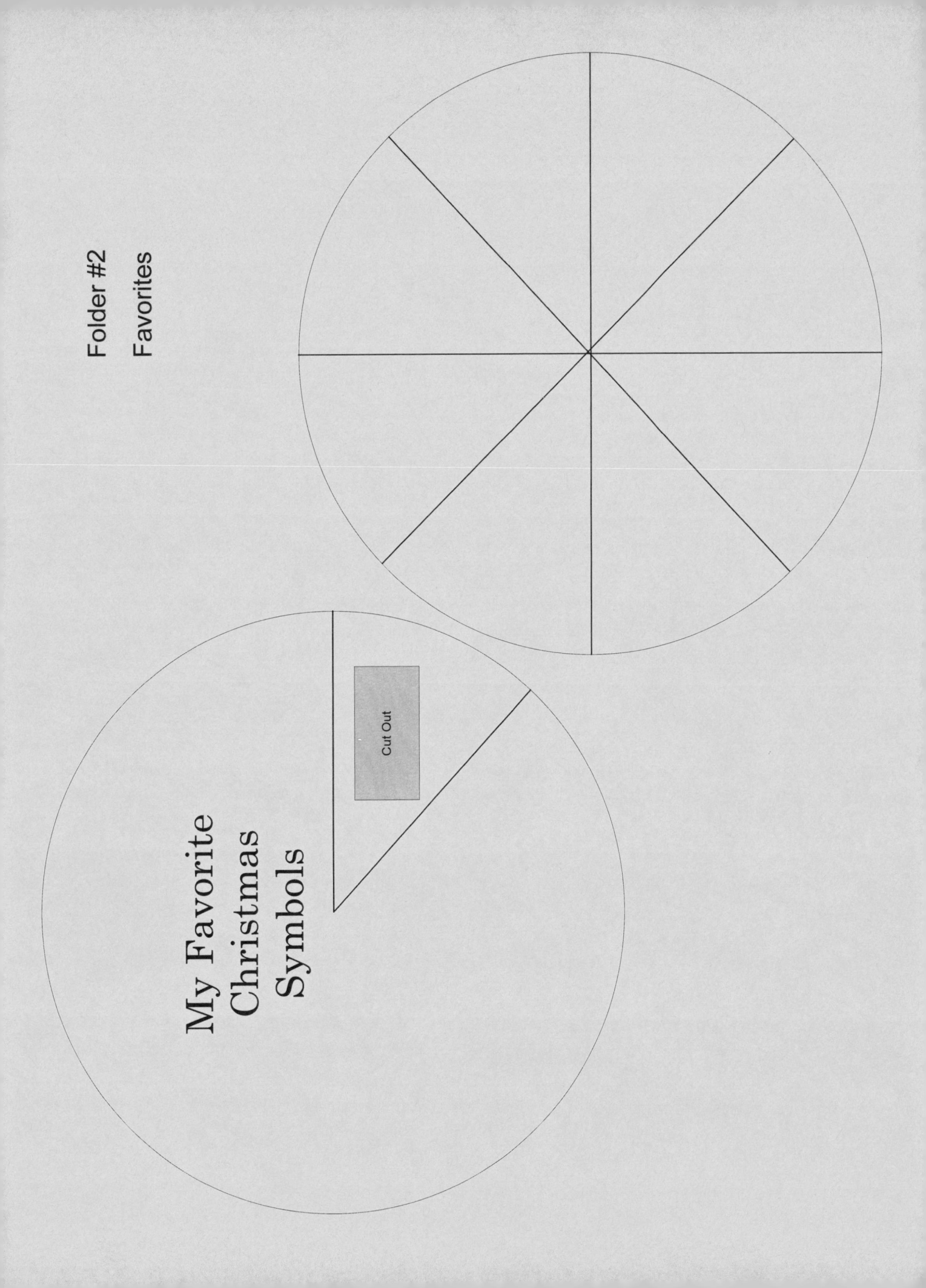

Folder #2

Favorites

Cut Out

My Favorite
Christmas
Symbols

Folder #3

Complete the Tree

Color/Paper Suggestion:

Print on white paper

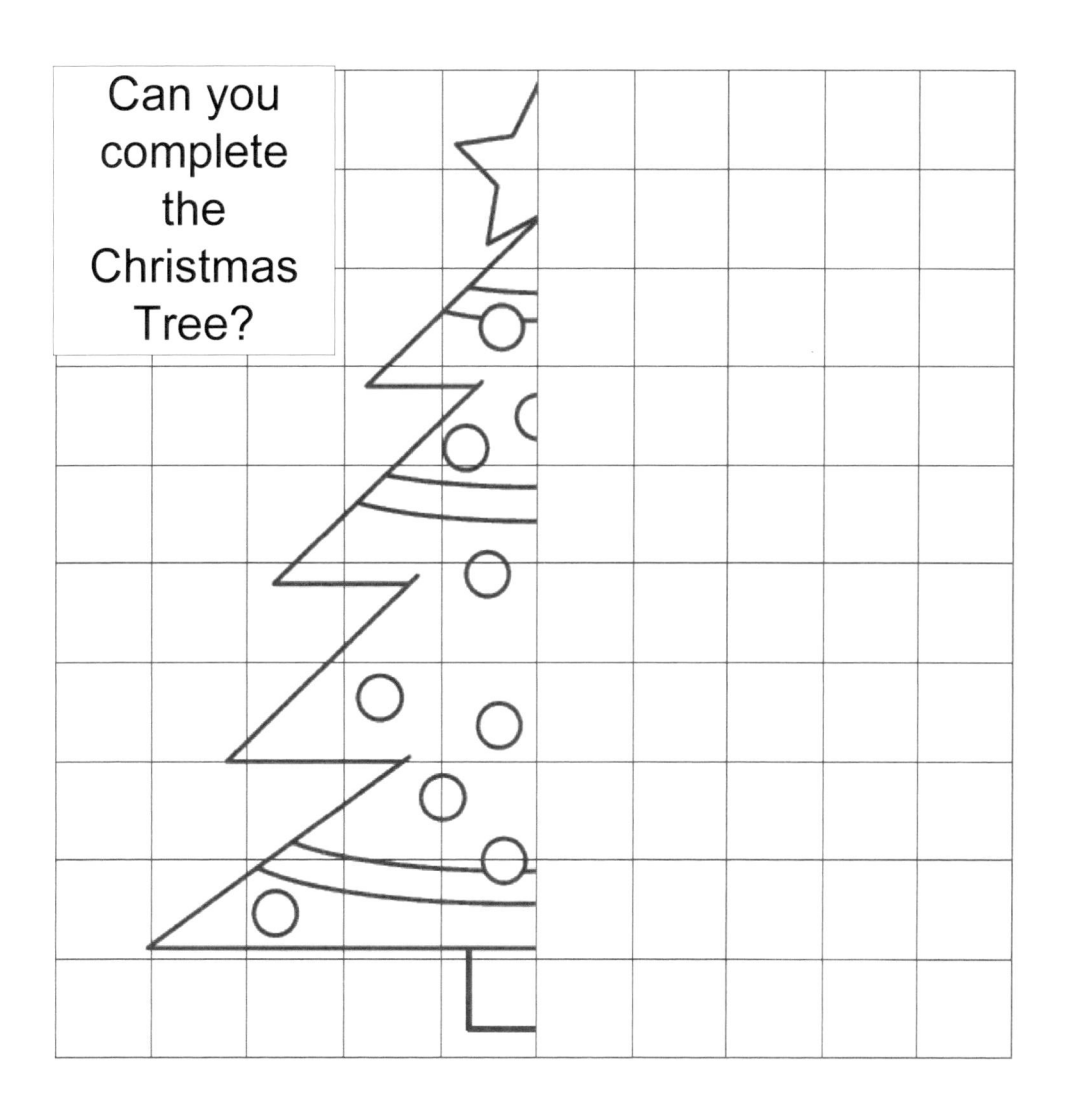

Can you complete the Christmas Tree?

Folder #3

*Complete the Tree

*Xmas

Candles

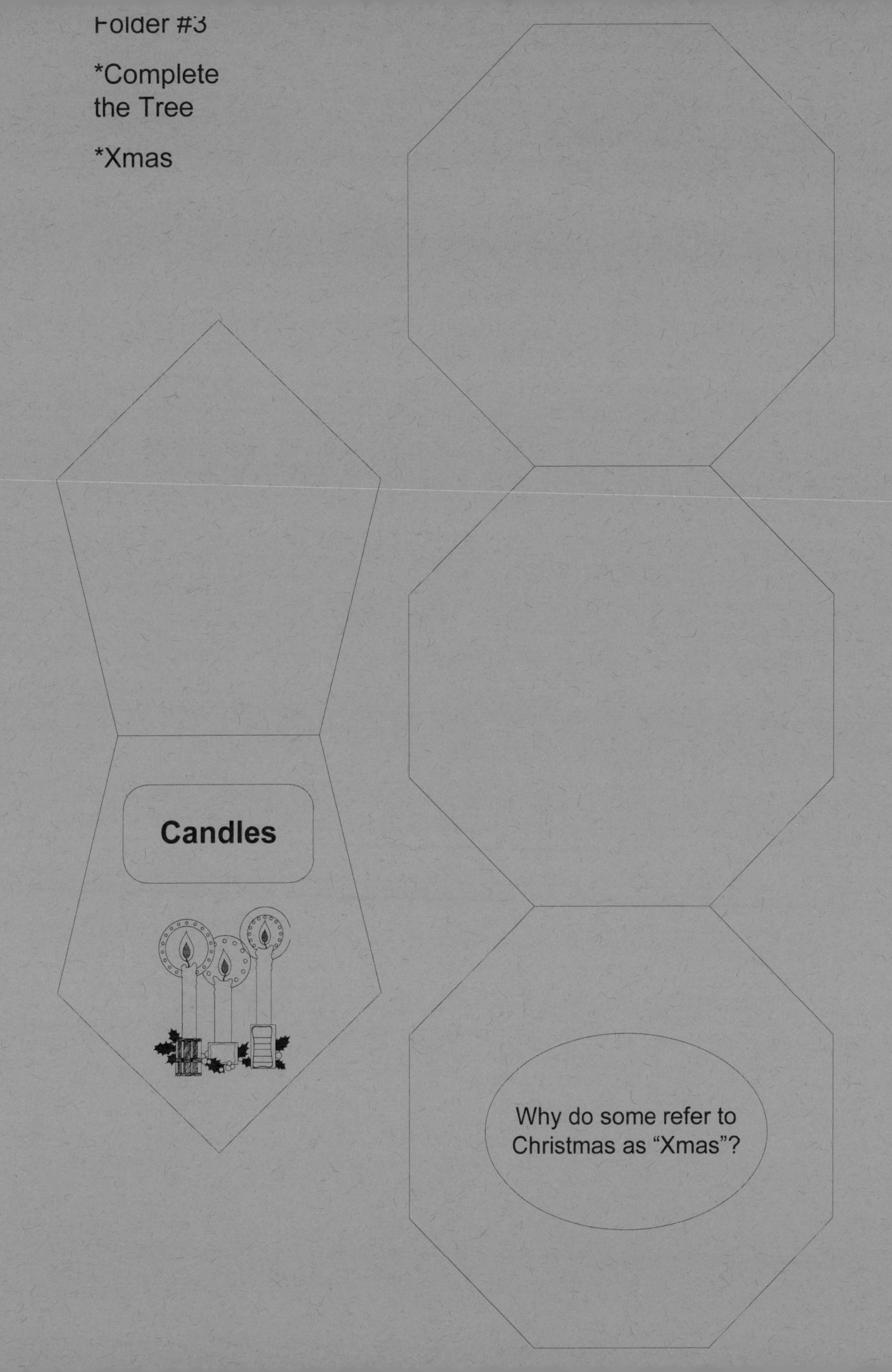

Why do some refer to Christmas as "Xmas"?

Folder #3

Advent

What is Advent, and what are Advent Wreaths?

Folder #3

Plants

Holly

Mistletoe

Poinsettia

CHRISTMAS PLANTS

The
Wreath

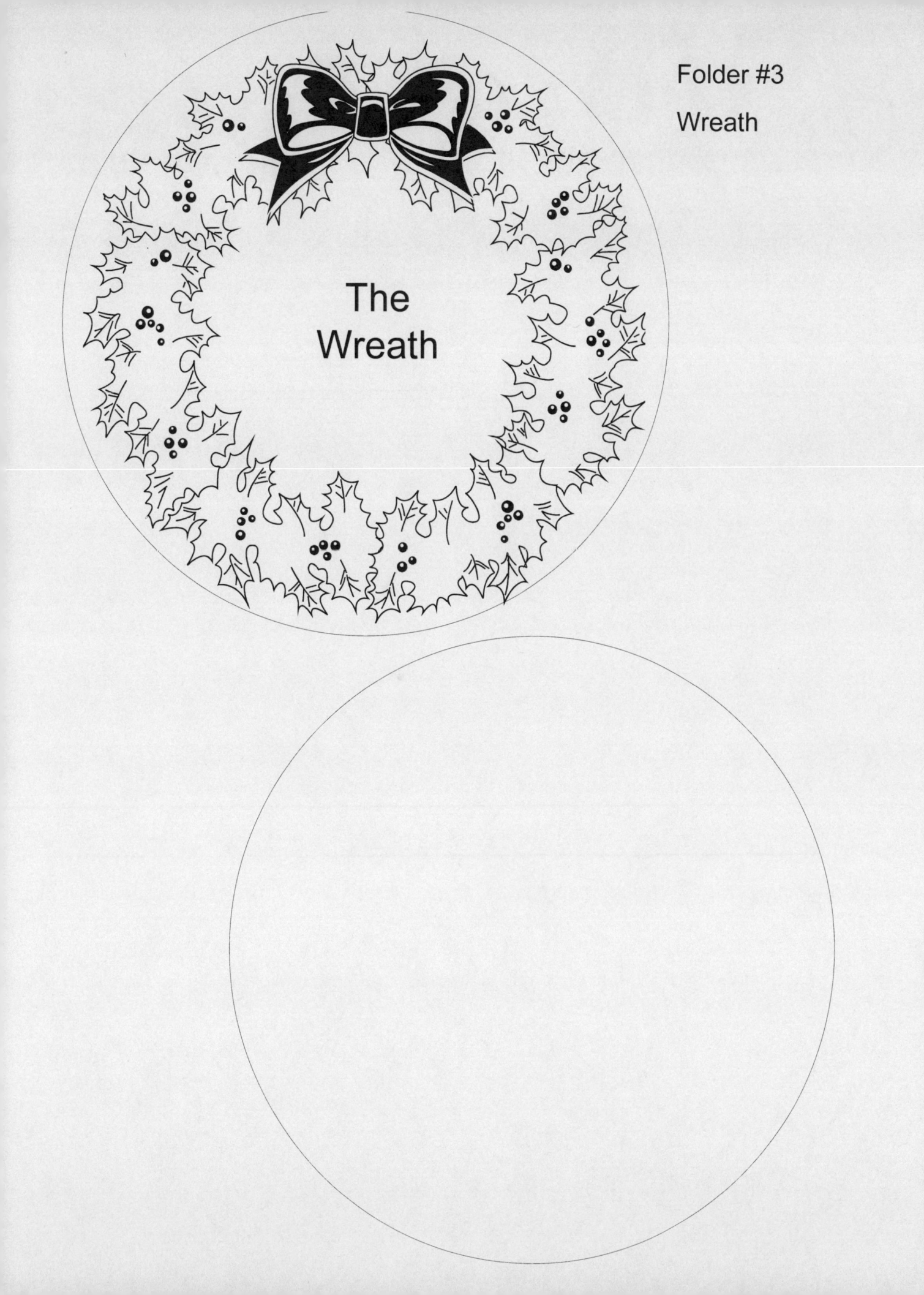

Folder #3

Wreath

Folder #3

Candy Cane

The Legend of The Candy Cane

Color/Paper Suggestion:

Print on white paper with colored ink

Folder #3

Gift Giving

Gift Giving

Folder #3
Crackers

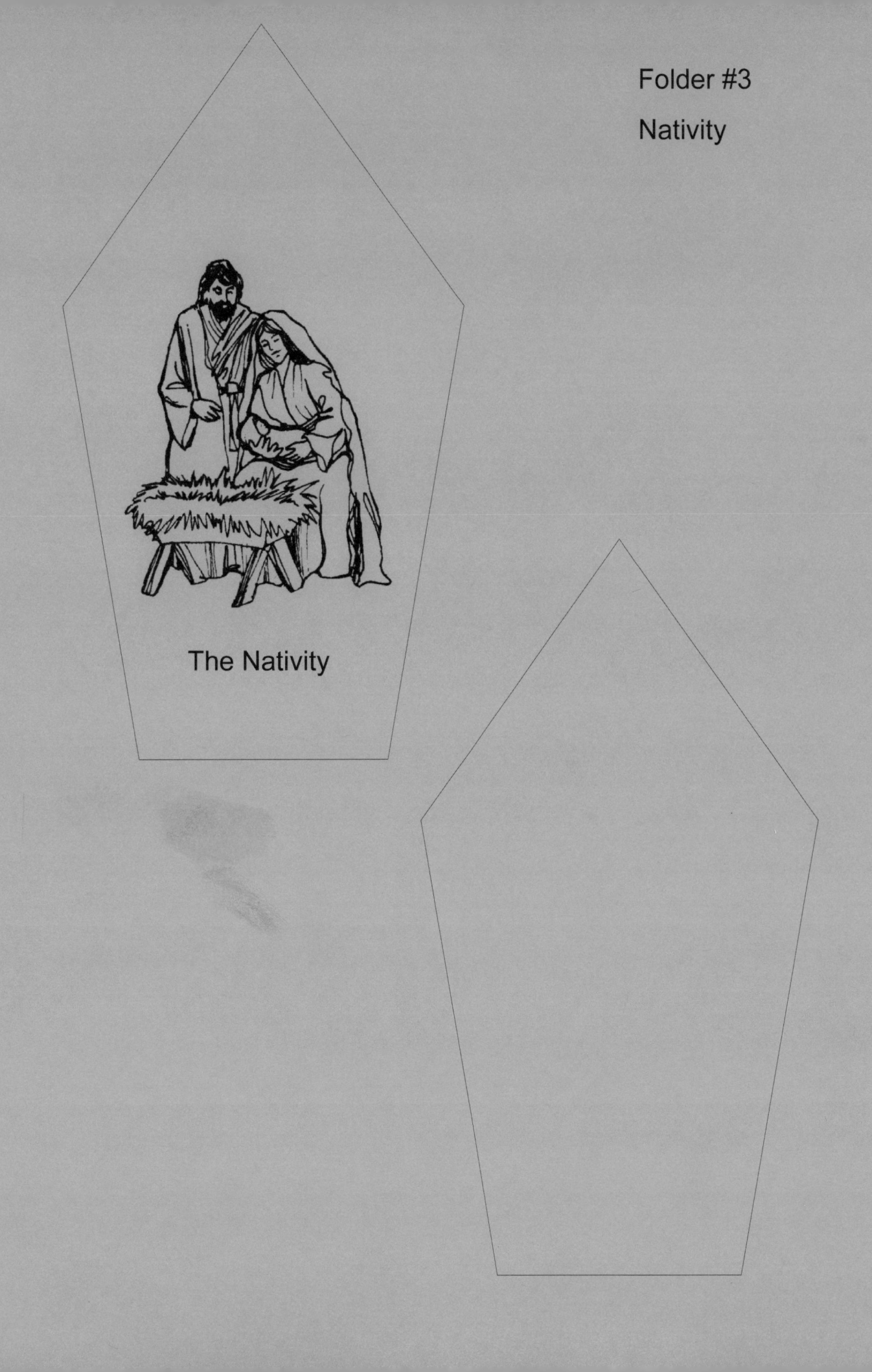

Folder #3

Nativity

The Nativity